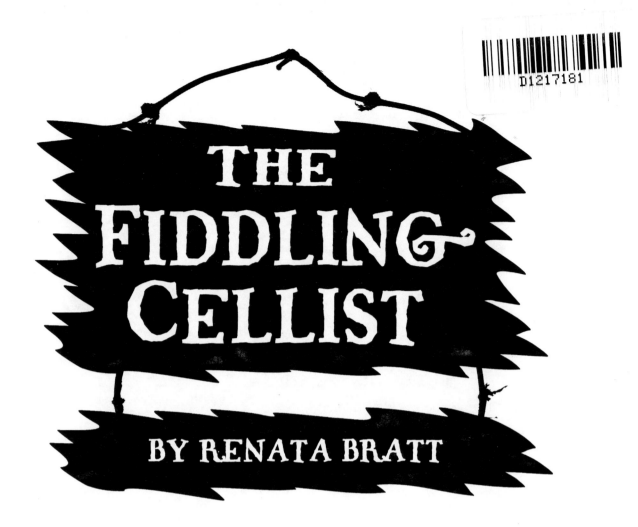

THE FIDDLING CELLIST

BY RENATA BRATT

1 2 3 4 5 6 7 8 9 0

© 2005 BY MEL BAY PUBLICATIONS, INC., PACIFIC, MO 63069.

Visit us on the Web at www.melbay.com — E-mail us at email@melbay.com

TABLE OF CONTENTS

INDEX OF CD TRACKS

Note: CD tracks in the text will be shown like this:

 Track 32

INDEX OF MUSIC EXAMPLES

Note: Music examples in the text will be shown like this: ♪♩ Example 32.

INTRODUCTION

This book is primarily for cellists who can already play pretty well – intermediate level and beyond. I let my students who have been playing for about a year play some of these tunes. Other tunes are best learned by students who have been playing for two or three years and more. Some of the tunes are challenging to cellists – they shift up to fourth position and require fast string-crossing – because violinists are responsible for transmitting most of this music and their strings are tuned a fifth above ours. Pieces that might be easy on the violin can be a lot more difficult on the cello, but all of these tunes are also played by mandolin players, guitarists, banjo players, dobro players – all sorts of instruments. I have tried to make versions of the tunes that are cello friendly.

If you are a beginner you can use this book by learning to play simple bass accompaniments. If you are an advanced cellist, you will get a great technical workout from these tunes when you work them up to speed. For all levels of cellists, your right hand will benefit from the bowing patterns and string crossings and your left hand will become used to playing note patterns quickly and accurately.

You can use this book in a variety of ways: you can learn the tunes – 18 great fiddle tunes in a variety of styles. You can learn how to accompany (play backup), providing harmony and bass lines for all occasions. You can learn how to improvise in fiddle and bluegrass music. And you can learn some music theory and harmony along the way.

I began playing fiddle tunes on the cello after a life-changing week at the Mark O'Connor Fiddle Conference. I went there to play jazz and left determined to play these beautiful and exciting tunes on the cello. After performing and teaching fiddle tunes to cellists around the country I realized that a book just for cellists, by a cellist, was needed.

Though it may be new to bluegrass, the cello has been around popular music since the seventeenth century. The cello has a great sound for fiddle music and can play a few different roles – a lead instrument playing tunes, a bass instrument playing bass lines, and a chordal instrument playing the backup harmony. When a cellist participates in a fiddle jam, they never have to stop playing no matter what instrument joins the jam!

USING THIS BOOK

You will find a lot of explanation during the section for each tune. If you want, skip the explanations and learn the tunes from the CD. Then go back and learn how to accompany and/or improvise. You can learn in your own style and at your own pace. Also, the tunes are performed much slower at the beginning of the CD. You might want to speed them up once you learn them. Tunes later in the book are performed at a quicker pace. Have fun!

ACKNOWLEDGEMENTS

Thanks to Mark O'Connor – a true inspiration to all; to Darol Anger for advising me to write this book, listening and helping with lots of my versions of these tunes (and consistently playing the music that I love); and to all of the great players who taught me these tunes, live or on recordings.

Thanks to my cello students here at home and my fiddling cello classes at the Colorado Suzuki Institute, the South Carolina Suzuki Institute and the Mark O'Connor Fiddle Conference. All of you encouraged me tremendously with your voracious appetite and love for these fiddle tunes.

Thanks also to my colleagues who reviewed this book for me—Glen Campbell, cellist with the San Diego Symphony and a Suzuki teacher; Christine Harrington, cellist and string teacher in the Cranston, Rhode Island school district; and David Hollender, bassist with the Boston Philharmonic and ensemble teacher at Berklee College. Any and all mistakes in this book are my own.

Special thanks to Jim Lewin for teaching, playing, and recording with me and to my husband, Lee Ray, for his editing and heaps of encouragement and help.

WORKING WITH *LIBERTY*

This is a duet arrangement of the fiddle tune Liberty. I learned this tune from Rushad Eggleston, a great bluegrass cellist. Although it is arranged in common time (4/4), the beat is really felt in two. So even though it looks slow, it should be played pretty fast, about m.m. 116 for the half note! Listen to the CD example before you play to hear how the tune sounds and to see how fast this should go. In a real jam session, this would probably be played even faster.

Track 1. *Liberty Duet*
Example 1: *Liberty for Two Cellos*

6

Liberty Duet

Listen to CD Track 1 a few times so that the tune of *Liberty* is in your ear. See if you can sing along with the CD. When you first play the tune, try playing without the printed music. See how much of the tune you can play before you look at the music. You don't have to play every note perfectly – just try to get the general contour of the piece. Then, if you like, play the top line of *Liberty Duet* (the tune).

Chords and associated scales used in *Liberty*

Now let's think about *Liberty* another way. For practicing purposes (so that you can play bass lines and fiddle tune improvisations based on the tune), here is a chart (written music) of the three chords and their associated scales that are used in this tune. As you can see in the tune chart above (♩♩ Example 1), the chords are notated with the letter names of the roots (the bottom note of the chord) written above the staff. The chords are written over the beats on which they should be played. Chords carry over to the next measure when no other chords appear. The chords are formed from triads, three notes stacked in intervals of a third. All of the chords in this tune are major chords. When applied to chords, the term "major" means that the first third above the root is a major third. Almost everyone associates or hears different qualities in the various musical intervals in melodies and chords. For instance, the major third often sounds bright, energetic and happy though it can also suggest relaxation and conclusion. These are just words of course. Music is much richer and more complex.

Theory Tip: All of the chords in *Liberty* are based on the D major Scale (the scale starting on the note D and having two sharps – F♯ and C♯). For example, right at the beginning of measure 1, the letter "D" appears at the top of the chart. This notation means that you use the chord built on the note D, adding the thirds F♯ and A.

Play the D major scale with the CD or the printed music or both. Then, you can play from G to G and from A to A using the same pitches as those for D major.

 Track 2. D, G and A scales
♩♩ **Example 2**. *Liberty* chords and scales

Notice in measures 4, 5, and 6, the G scale sounds a bit different than a G major scale. It has a C♯ in it! That's because this kind of G scale is built on the fourth note of the D major scale.

Theory Tip: The resulting scale is called a *Lydian* scale – a major scale with a sharp 4 (in this case, C♯). A neat sound, different than the basic major scale.

Theory Tip: Look at the next chord in measure 7. The A has a 7 next to it. That 7 means that the chord includes a flat seven – use a regular major scale with the seven (G♯) dropped down one half step (G). You don't need to remember all of this theory though. Just play all of the scales using an F♯ and a C♯; the key of D Major.

Accompanying *Liberty*

An easy way to accompany this tune with a good bass line is by using the traditional bluegrass style: pizzicato notes playing just the root of the chord (the bottom note – also the note named as the chord) and the fifth of the scale. Always play the root as low on your instrument as you can. This provides a firm anchoring pitch for the group. Notice in the following example that the root is always on beat one and the fifth is always on beat three.

Track 3. *Liberty* bass line, using the root and fifth of the chord
Example 3. *Liberty* bass line

9

Theory Tip: You need to know that you can move from the root of the chord to the fifth of the chord by either ascending or descending. For instance, the motion from G to D in measure 3 is ascending. In measure 4 the same *musical* motion is descending. Both of these measures use the same pitches, but the D in measure 4 is an octave lower than the D in measure 5. If you're going down in pitch from the root of the chord to the fifth of the chord, you are going down the interval of a fourth. Fourths are upside-down (or inverted) fifths, and vice versa. That's why measure 4 and 12 are going down by fourths. Get used to this sound and how you finger the fifths and fourths.

Performance Tip: If there are two chords in a measure, just play the root of each chord. A bluegrass bass line sounds particularly good if you are playing in a jam session without a bass player and with other chording instruments, such as a mandolin or guitar. This easy rhythm really propels a group and is much appreciated by all of the players. Learn to play it cheerfully and well! You might think the part is too simple, but it really works well for the group. When accompanying, more notes are not always better.

Now listen to CD Track 1 again. This time listen to the second cello part. After you've listened to the track a few times, read through the bottom part of *Liberty Duet* (♪ ♩ Example 1) This is another type of backup.

Theory Tip: In the duet arrangement, the bottom cello is playing an arpeggio – the notes of the chords played one after another rather than all at the same time. This type of pattern works well when playing without another chording instrument. It uses simple triadic harmony, the root, the tenth (major third of the chord), the fifth (where a bluegrass bass player would play it) and the tenth again. Play through that second line part and get the feel of these roots and fifths with the added tenth. Except when the root is on an open string, I usually just play the same fingering (1-3-1-3) with my first finger on the bottom string playing the root of the chord. I bar across the two lower strings with my first finger (keeping my first finger straight and letting my left elbow hang down so that I can use the weight of my arm to keep the string down) and put my third finger on the string above them. Then shift when needed, using the same fingering, the way that guitarists bar chords.

Improvising with *Liberty*

Traditional players often base their improvisations on features of the tune they are playing. In the second measure, *Liberty* uses lots of notes from the first three notes of the "D" scale. Also, as a point of information, traditional players usually play fairly constant eighth note patterns with a few quarter notes thrown in at high points in the tune. For this improvisation exercise, play eighth notes from the first three notes of each scale whenever there are quarter notes in the measure. Where are those measures? There are quarter notes in measures 1, 3, 5, 8, 12 and 16.

For this sample improvisation, I have used exactly the same eighth note patterns in the measures that contained quarter notes. First, just play those measures. The printed music has rests in the other measures. Think about the chord changes or the patterns you are creating during the measures of rest.

Track 4. Beginning improvisation

♪♩ **Example 4**. *Liberty* Improvisation

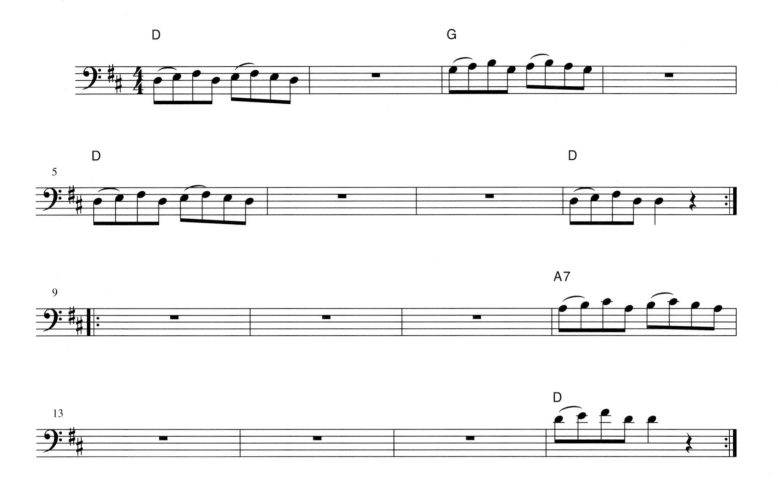

After you have tried this out, use just those first three notes of each scale – starting with the root or third and then playing the notes in any order – to play your own improvisation during those measures. Use CD Track 3 which is the basic backup track for this piece.

Track 5. Improvisation with tune fragments

Listen to CD Track 5, an example of using the beginning improvisation pattern together with measures of the tune. Either using the printed music or your own ear, play the beginning improvisation again and instead of resting, play the tune as you have already learned it. I composed this variation using lots of repeated music because bluegrass players like to play the original parts of the tune fairly frequently. When you are practicing or performing, you don't have to use these patterns for improvising. Make up your own!

♩♩ **Example 5**. *Liberty* Improvisation with tune fragments

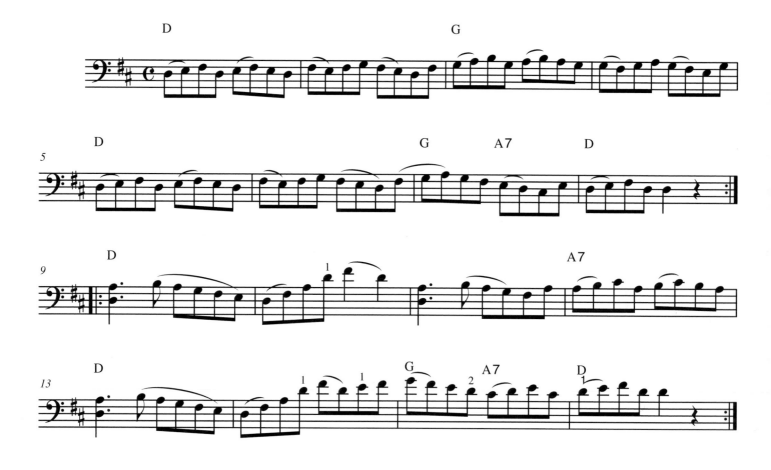

WORKING WITH *CHEROKEE SHUFFLE*

This great old tune has more measures than usual in its second section. I first learned it from Jim Lewin, the fine bluegrass guitarist you hear performing on the CD.

Theory Tip: Most traditional tunes have 8 bars that repeat in each section but this one has 10 in the B section. The sections of a tune, which are often eight bars long, are designated "A" for the first section, "B" for the second section and so on. As a shortcut, musicians can then refer to the various sections by letter as in, "let's start on the second time through the 'A' section."

Before you start playing, listen to the tune a few times on the CD. Sing it through as soon as you have the tune in your ear. Try to play through as much of it as you can without the printed music. Because it is in the key of A (three sharps – F♯, C♯ and G♯), remember to use extended position (a whole step between your first and second finger – second and fourth finger play 1/2 step higher than usual) for all of the pitches on the C, D and G strings. Here is the chart.

Cherokee Shuffle Duet

Here are the chords and the corresponding scales for *Cherokee Shuffle*.

Track 7. *Cherokee Shuffle* chords with scales

♪♩ **Example 7**. *Cherokee Shuffle* chords and scales

Theory Tip: Again, as in many traditional tunes, all of the chords and their scales are based on the key of the tune, in this case A major. Remember, A major has three sharps in it – F♯, C♯ and G♯. That G♯ can be tough on the cello, but it's good to learn this key well because a lot of fiddle tunes are in A (a key that violinists like).

Theory Tip: Notice that the scale for the D chord, which is based on the fourth note of the A scale, has a G♯ in it. That's the raised 4th and so the chord D in the key of A uses the Lydian scale. This is the same type of scale as that for the G chord in *Liberty* (♪♩ Example 2).

The F♯min ("min" is short for minor) scale is based on the sixth note of the A scale. Such a scale, with a minor third, a flat sixth and a flat seventh is called an *Aeolian* scale. It's also called a *natural minor* scale. It has a minor third in the first triad. Some people think that minor chords sound sad. Do you? Learning to associate the feelings and expressive characters of melodies and chords will help you improvise and perform all types of music better.

Accompanying Cherokee Shuffle

Now make your own bluegrass bass accompaniment. If you've forgotten how, review the bass accompaniment for *Liberty*. The recording for this example will also help you remember. CD Track 8 demonstrates the bluegrass bass accompaniment.

14

Practice your arpeggio accompaniment for this tune using the given chords. This style is shown in the duet Cello 2 part (♩♩ Example 6). Listen to that example (CD Track 6) and notice that some of the bass notes are used to connect in step-wise motion (as in a scale) to the next chord. Such connections occur in measures 3, 4, 6 and 16.

Another way to accompany is an idea based on a rock and roll-type driving bass riff. The accents are placed on what are sometimes called the "Charleston" beats – the one and the "and" of beat two. Listen to the CD example a few times (CD Track 9). Sing the rhythm with the track. Try to play the notes without using the printed music. Then play with the music. Practice this until it sounds confident and correct; the syncopation can be a little harder than it looks.

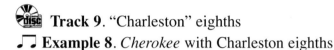 **Track 9**. "Charleston" eighths
♩♩ **Example 8**. *Cherokee* with Charleston eighths

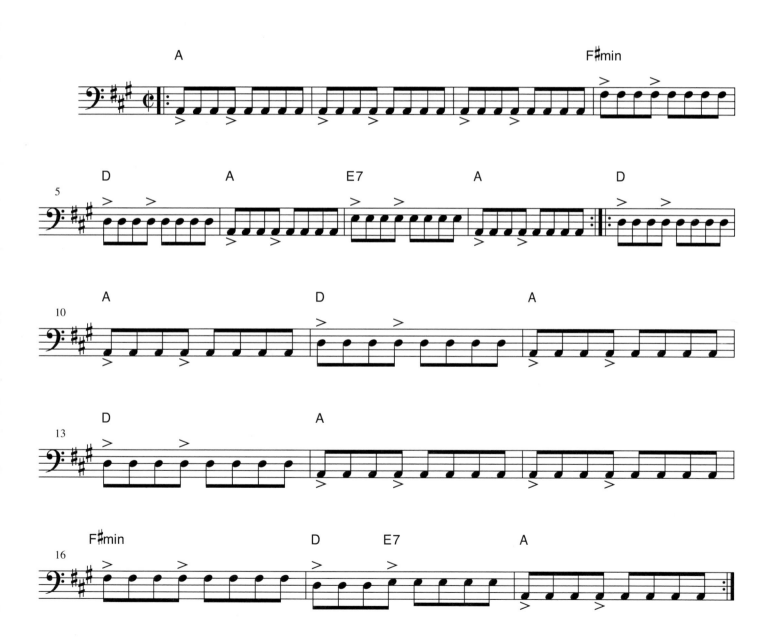

You shouldn't use this syncopation pattern in a strictly traditional setting, but everyone else likes to hear this occasionally, and it's fun to play. Use a very small amount of bow on the eighth notes. Don't try this with a really fast fiddler like Mark O'Connor though; he can actually play a tune faster than you can play these repeated eighth notes!

Improvising with *Cherokee Shuffle*

For this improvisation, simply play the melody up an octave. This technique is used as part of an improvised section by many fine players, sometimes taking the tune (or parts of it) up an octave, sometimes down. Played in the upper octave, the *Cherokee Shuffle* sounds particularly powerful on the cello. Listen to the CD track a few times. Try playing without the printed music first.

Track 10. *Cherokee Shuffle* played an octave above the original

Example 9. *Cherokee Shuffle*, an Octave Higher

Cherokee Shuffle
An Octave Higher

Now using this same improvisational device, go back to *Liberty* and play through the B section, measures 10 through 19, an octave below where it's printed. That's a nice low sound, and fun to play as a variation. Rushad Eggleston refers to these low variations as "Grumbly".

Here's a more modern version of the *Cherokee Shuffle*. The eclectic and amazing fiddler Darol Anger showed me this one. Use this variation when you want to impress your new bluegrass friends with your up-to-the-minute style.

Track 11. Modern *Cherokee Shuffle*

♫♩ **Example 10**. *Cherokee Shuffle, as Played by Darol Anger*

Cherokee Shuffle
as Played by Darol Anger

WORKING WITH *STAR OF THE COUNTY DOWN*

Star of the County Down is a beautiful Irish ballad in 3/4 time that I first learned with my playing buddy, violinist Ben Blechman. It's in a minor key, as are many traditional slow waltzes. This tune is in A minor, a key with no flats or sharps. Notice that in the B section (after the repeat) the tune goes into C Major, the relative major of A minor. That means it is in the major key that also has no sharps or flats. First listen, sing and then play through the first cello part of this tune with the recording a few times. Isn't it lovely? Because it is in a minor key, it sounds sad, but the words of the song itself are happy – a pretty girl goes to the fair, meets a nice guy and they live happily ever after.

Track 12. *Star of the County Down Duet*
Example 11. *Star of the County Down Duet*

Star of the County Down
Duet

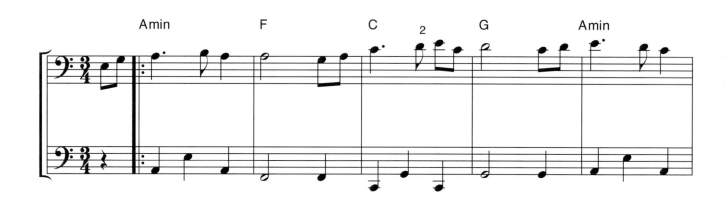

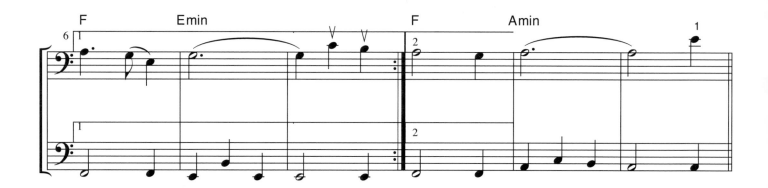

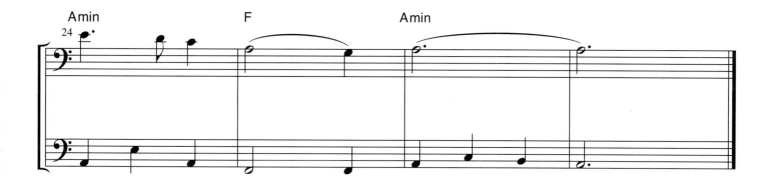

Next are the chords and the scales that go with them for the *Star of the County Down*. Play through these scales with the CD. Listen to the scales that go with this minor key. Many of the ballads, waltzes and slow tunes in fiddle music are in minor keys.

Track 13. *Star of the County Down* chords and the scales

Example 12. *Star of the County Down* chords and scales

Theory Tip: As in our previous tunes, all of the chords and scales are formed from the notes of one scale. In this case, it is the scale of A minor. So if you improvise over this tune, keep in mind that you need to stay in that key area. It has no sharps or flats, no matter what note you start from. *Star of the County Down* has more chord changes than we've had in the previous pieces, but luckily it's nice and slow. Play through the scales and chords of this tune. Go ahead and arpeggiate the chords. Aren't they pretty?

Accompanying *Star of the County Down*

For these slower tunes, sometime it's nice to play long tones in the bass. Here's a chart of all of the bass notes played as dotted half notes. Listen to how it makes the melody sound.

Track 14. Long bass notes with guitar accompaniment and tune

♫ **Example 13**. *Star of the County Down* long bass notes

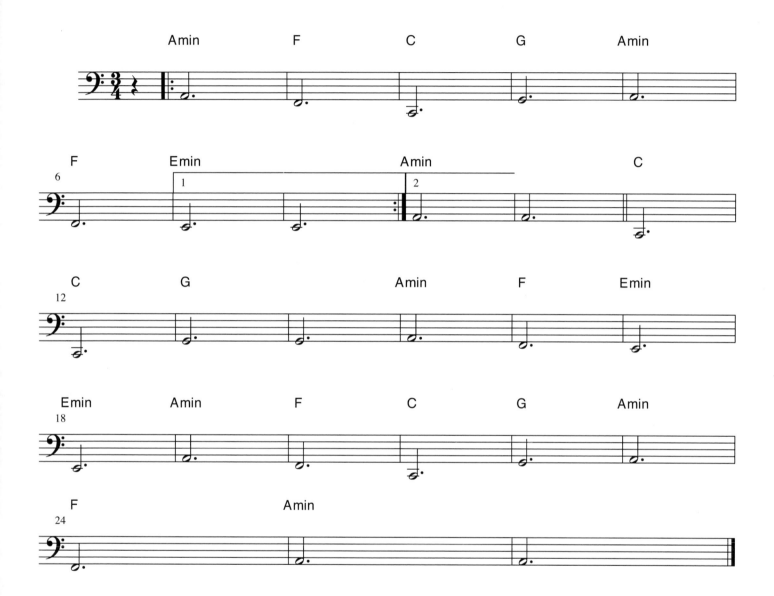

In the duet arrangement, the second cello plays a bass line using a two-measure rhythmic pattern. Play through that second cello part now if you haven't already (CD Track 12).

Theory Tip: In the A section, the first measure of the accompaniment pattern uses three quarter notes alternating the root and fifth of each chord. The second measure uses a half note/quarter note rhythm played with just the root of the chord. In the B section (after the repeat signs), the tune seems to sound better with the three quarter notes per measure bass line. Also, you may have noticed that the pattern changes at the end of each section. The root goes to the third of the chord rather than the fifth. That's one way you can help the person playing the melody or taking a solo hear the difference between sections. Making each section distinct like this is musically satisfying and very helpful to the other musicians.

Try developing your own bass line by playing along with the following recording featuring only the tune with guitar accompaniment. Look at the long bass notes study (p. 21) for chord information, and play with a steady beat using CD Track 15. Use the arpeggio information from the chord study if you'd like.

 Track 15. *Star of the County Down* with no bass

Improvising with *Star of the County Down*

For this improvisation study, you will learn some different ways of decorating the melody. In Celtic tunes, many of the grace notes (sometimes called "cuts") are based on bagpipe licks. The bagpipe can never play two of the same notes in a row because the player has no way of stopping the tone. So, to show the difference between two of the same tones in a row, the piper will put in a quick extra note, a grace note between the two. The other decorating notes in this study are mostly scale-type passages that connect notes a third or more apart, and some of the note decorations are there just because they sound pretty. Usually, grace notes are slurred to the following note with the bow. Listen to the CD track a few times. Sing and imitate what you hear. Play through this example and see how you like it.

Track 16. *Star of the County Down* with grace notes
♪♩ **Example 14**. *Star of the County Down* with grace notes

Star of the County Down
with grace notes

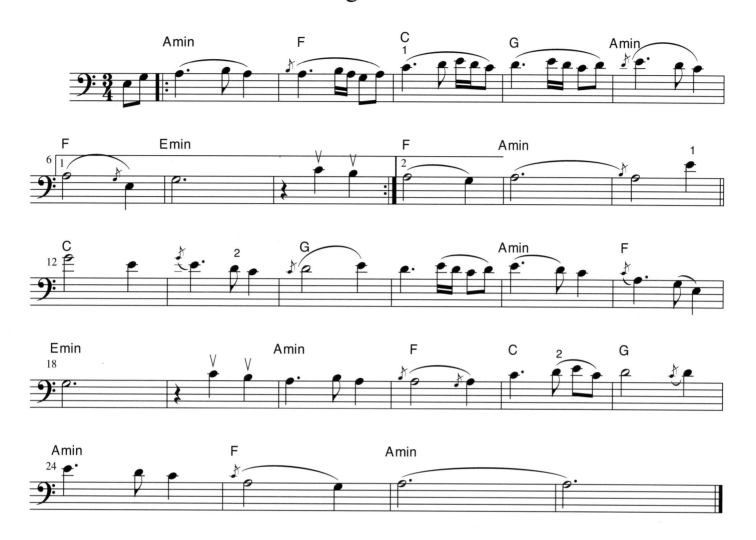

Try out your own ideas about decorating the melody with grace notes. Try playing the second section (m. 12–19) an octave down and see how that sounds. Use CD Track 17.

Track 17. *Star of the County Down* backup track

Working with *Big Scioty*

The Scioty is a big brown river that flows past Columbus, Ohio. It was called the Scioty and the Sciota by settlers and is now formally known as the Scioto River. Bluegrass guitarist Russ Barenberg taught it to just about everybody and they in turn taught it to everyone else, and here it is.

Big Scioty is in the very cello-friendly key of G major. Notice that the key signature has just one sharp, F♯. Don't forget to listen to the CD track frequently before you play this or any other tune in the book. Sing through the tune before you play it. Play as much of the tune without the printed music as you can, then look at the music.

🄌 **Track 18**. *Big Scioty Duet*
♪♩ **Example 15**. *Big Scioty Duet*

Big Scioty
Duet

Accompanying *Big Scioty*

Find the chords and scales for this tune below (♪♩ Example 17). Before you play the Cello 2 part, figure out your own bluegrass bass notes again (root and fifth of the chord, pizzicato) according to the suggested chords in the duet. Play through the tune with the bluegrass bass using CD Track 19. Now play through the tune with your arpeggio accompaniment style, again using the given chord symbols.

 Track 19. *Big Scioty* backup track with bluegrass bass

Performance Tip: In the measures with two chords in them – measures 1 and 3 – just play the root and tenth (the major third) of each chord. Use very little bow and keep your bow on the string during the string crossings. Just rock over the string you don't use. And finally, try using the Charleston eighths on the roots of the chords. Read through the explanation for the *Cherokee Shuffle* rocking bass notes (♪♩ Example 8) if you've forgotten the details

Here's a new idea for bass accompaniment, a chuggin' bass rhythm that is our introduction to the rhythm of the double shuffle string crossing technique. This style uses a higher pitch (the third note of the scale) to emphasize every third eighth note. Try this syncopation as printed (♪♩ Example 16), first using accented notes on one pitch, then with every third note played up to the third of the chord. Which is easier to do?

Notice that the accented pattern in measure 5 and 6 is different than that in measure 1 and 2. Measures 1 and 2 (and 3 and 4) are a two-measure rhythmic pattern. Measures 5 and 6 (and 7 and 8) are a one-measure rhythmic pattern. However you play it, it's a great syncopated sound.

Example 16. *Big Scioty* chuggin' bass rhythm

The Cello 2 part (♪♩ Example 15) in the *Big Scioty Duet* uses this double shuffle sound and includes a double stop a fifth above the root (first finger barred across on the string above) for even more chugging sound. Keep your fingers curved and watch out for measure 14. Play this measure in the second position. I have eliminated the quick chord change in the first measure (G to D) to keep the pattern going. It won't disturb anyone playing a bluegrass bass part at all.

Listen to CD Track 18 a few times. Now try it out!

Improvising with *Big Scioty*

Another type of scale that is often used by fiddle players is the *pentatonic* scale.

Theory Tip: Pentatonic means "five-tone", so these are five-note scales. They have a neat sound all their own and can sometimes seem a little less fussy than a full major or minor scale. Here are the pentatonic scales that go with the chords in *Big Scioty*.

Track 20. *Big Scioty* chords and pentatonic scales

♪♩ **Example 17**. *Big Scioty* pentatonics

You may have noticed that each scale has six notes, not five. That's because these scales (like the seven note scales you have already learned) also include the note which is the root of the scale on the top. G goes to G, D to D, and so on. If you leave out that octave root note, there are five notes in the scale. Notice that the pentatonic pattern is different for minor scales and major scales. How are they different? The minor pentatonic scales start with a skip, emphasizing the minor third. They also use the fourth and seventh degrees of the scale. In addition to the root and the major third, the major pentatonic scales use the second and sixth degrees of the scale and skip the fourth and seventh.

For the following improvisational study, you will find pentatonic scales replacing the regular (step-wise) scales in the tune. Try out this version and see how it sounds.

Track 21. *Big Scioty* pentatonic improvisation
Example 18. *Big Scioty* improvisation with pentatonic scales

Try making up your own pentatonic improvisation using CD Track 19. Use the notes from the pentatonic scales in any order, but try to start each pattern with a note from the chord (the root, third or fifth). You can also try starting patterns with notes that are not in the chord. Which patterns do you like better? There is no right answer, just your own ear.

Remember, you don't have to play all of the time. If you feel like you're getting behind, just rest or play long notes! For fun, go back and use this same improvisational device in *Liberty*. The D major pentatonic scales for *Liberty* are found later in this book in *Fisher's Hornpipe* (Example 21). Now try another variation by playing the A section from *Big Scioty* an octave above.

WORKING WITH *RUBBER DOLLY*

Here's a simple fiddle tune (just eight bars!) that illustrates a variety of fiddling variations that you can use when improvising on other tunes. My friend, the fabulous fiddler Crystal Plohman, showed me this one away out in Colorado on a hillside in Snowmass. The lyrics for this tune are also used in an old jump-rope rhyme: "My mother told me / if I was goodie / that she would buy me / a rubber dolly" and so on.

Track 22. *Rubber Dolly* with variations
Listen to the tune a few times. Now try singing it. How much of it can you play without using the printed music? At first, just play the first 8 bar section. This is the tune. Shift to 2nd position in measure 6 so that you can play the E and don't forget that the C on the G string is a high one – it's C#! As you learn the variations, be sure to stay in extended position in measures 27 and 28.

♩♩ **Example 19**. *Rubber Dolly*

Rubber Dolly

Because it is in the key of A major, the scales and chords for *Rubber Dolly* are the same as those in *Cherokee Shuffle*, though there is no F♯ minor in *Rubber Dolly*. Review those scales and chords before proceeding to the accompaniment section.

Accompanying *Rubber Dolly*

Review and practice all of the different bass lines styles that you have learned so far: bluegrass bass, arpeggio accompaniment, Charleston rhythm, and the chuggin' bass double shuffle.

Improvising with *Rubber Dolly*

The first variation at measure 12 is the "shuffle" rhythm. The second variation at measure 22 uses a "slide" style, first playing a note a half step below the final note in a more elaborate version of the shuffle. The third and final variation at measure 32 uses the regular double shuffle with alternating strings, just like the bass notes in *Big Scioty's* Cello 2 part. Try out your own variations for this tune using CD Track 23. Play in different octaves or use the first three to five notes of the scales that go with the chords (D, A, and E) in any order. Use pentatonic scales alternating with the different variation styles within each 8-bar phrase

Track 23. *Rubber Dolly* Backup

WORKING WITH *FISHER'S HORNPIPE*

Fisher's Hornpipe is played very frequently at jam sessions. I can't remember where I learned this one, but thanks to whoever it was who taught me!

 Track 24. *Fisher's Hornpipe Duet*

As always, listen to the CD track a few times first. Sing through the tune. Notice that the eighth notes in this piece are not played straight. They are played in "swing time." The first of each pair of eighth notes is a little bit longer than the second eighth note. It's almost a quarter note to eighth note triplet rhythm. Sing along with the recording a few times to get the feel of this rhythm. Many old-time fiddlers play all eighth notes with swing feel. The rest of us can pick and choose. Try playing this and other tunes in this book with swing eighths. Play *Fisher's Hornpipe* with straight eighths. How do you like the piece(s) best? There is no right answer – your own opinion is fine.

♪♩ **Example 20**. *Fisher's Hornpipe Duet*

Fisher's Hornpipe Duet

Accompanying *Fisher's Hornpipe*

Fisher's Hornpipe uses the same chords and scales as *Liberty*, since both are in the key of D major. Review (♪♪ Example 2) if needed.

There are two different types of bass lines in the second cello part. In the A section, use bluegrass bass with just the roots of the chords, since the chords change so frequently. In the B section, use the arpeggiated chords. Notice that the chords only change once per measure rather than two times in each measure as they do in the first section.

Try using a variety of bass lines, changing in each section, in this tune and in all of the previous tunes. Review all of the different styles you have learned.

Improvising with *Fisher's Hornpipe*

Here are the chords and pentatonic scales for *Fisher's Hornpipe*.

Track 25. *Fisher's Hornpipe* chords and pentatonic scales

Example 21. *Fisher's Hornpipe* pentatonics

Track 26. *Fisher's Hornpipe* pentatonic study

The first part of the *Fisher's Hornpipe* improvisation study uses the pentatonic scales that go with the chords in D major with some octave transposition of the tune. Listen to and play the study. The second part of the study uses the double shuffle rhythm to add rhythmic interest to the tune.

Example 22. *Fisher's Hornpipe Variations*

Fisher's Hornpipe
Variations

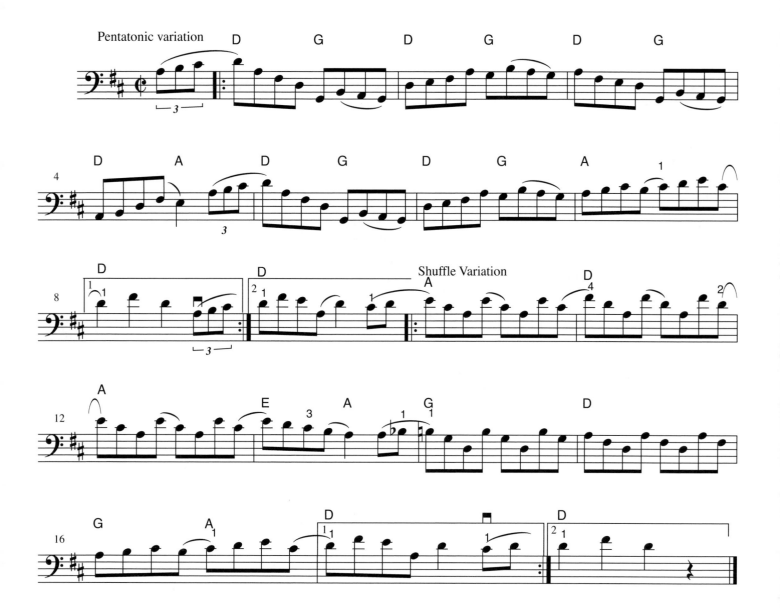

Make up your own pentatonic improvisation using CD Track 27. Getting a good feel for pentatonic scales will really help you with all types of improvisation. Use notes from the pentatonic scales instead of the shuffles for the second part of the tune (m.10–the end) and see how you like that sound.

Track 27. *Fisher's Hornpipe* backup

INTERLUDE: GETTING FURTHER INTO THE SOUND OF FIDDLING

You should know that I have used a somewhat classical cello sound when recording these tunes. This means that I used a strong, consistent tone – with not too much difference between individual notes – by keeping the contact point with my bow pretty much in the same place and bowing at a right angle to each string.

The contact point is the place between the fingerboard and the bridge where the bow contacts the string. Many fiddlers allow their bows to drift over the string because the bow is not kept at a right angle. Letting your bow drift to these different places on the string can produce sounds and notes that are quite different from each other. This adds a lot of variety and interest just in the sound of the bowing.

In order to hear more for yourself, listen to a lot of fiddle players, live or on recordings. Focus on the sounds of the bowing in addition to the notes and rhythms. Listen to a variety of recordings in different styles. Try to imitate the sounds that you hear on those recordings. If you can, get out to concerts by bluegrass, Celtic or Appalachian players. Watch the way they move. Live performances can be very rich sources of information if you set aside some time to look, listen and learn.

Watch the fiddler's bow arm – what are they doing? Watch the bow crossing the strings – does the arm look like it is tight or relaxed? Most fiddlers have amazingly relaxed right arms. That's one way they manage to get the bow over the strings so fast. Watch the amount of bow used (for fast passages this is often a surprisingly small amount of bow). Watch the bow placement on the strings. Is it always in the same place, or does it change? You can see and hear that you don't need to play all fiddle tunes with a focused sound. Notice that you don't have to play near the frog (where your hand holds the bow) all of the time. Playing over the fingerboard (*sul tasto*) or near the bridge (*ponticello*) yields different interesting sounds that you can use as part of your phrasing.

Watch the fiddle player's left hand – what are they doing? How are they placing their fingers? Listen to the slides, the intonation (Appalachian fiddlers play with a different type of intonation from classical players – it sounds ancient and cool!), the grace notes, and any improvisation you can hear.

When you are back home after the concert or after you have listened to a recording, play while imitating the sound and move the way that you remember the fiddle player moving. Try playing your fiddle tunes with a raspy sound. Play with your bow gliding on top of the string and not digging in at all. Then play with a focused sound and compare. Recording yourself will come in handy for this sort of effort since you can start, stop and play various techniques over again. Don't stop playing the way that you've learned to play: realize that you can add expressive sound in fiddle styles using various techniques.

Here are some of the fiddlers I listened to while preparing this book:

Old-time Fiddle: Tommy Jarrell, Bruce Molsky

Bluegrass: Kenny Baker, Stuart Duncan, Richard Greene, Mark O'Connor, Buddy Spicher, Scotty Stoneman

Texas Fiddling: Byron Berline, Johnny Gimble, Eck Robertson

Celtic: Liz Carroll, Alasdair Fraser, Natalie MacMaster, Bonnie Rideout

Newgrass: Darol Anger

Bands: Flatt and Scruggs, David Grisman Quintet, Bill Monroe and his Bluegrass Boys, Fiddlers 4

Fiddling Cellists: Nancy Blake, Rushad Eggleston, Natalie Haas, Abby Newton

---

WORKING WITH *DOWN IN THE WILLOW GARDEN*

I first heard and played this tune at a CD release party for Darol Anger's beautiful album, *Heritage*. It's a haunting murder ballad, as were many tunes from the frontier in the nineteenth century. Listen to the tune on the accompaniment CD and don't play this one too fast. You can even use a little vibrato on the long notes if you'd like.

Performance Tip: For most fiddle tunes, vibrato isn't used much. For one thing, the notes are too fast. Even the slower notes should not use too much vibrato (if any) because you must blend with musicians who don't use it. It's a good thing to reflect on the fact that using vibrato is not always stylistically appropriate. A lot of folk music requires tact with vibrato.

 Track 28. *Down in the Willow Garden Duet*

Listen to the tune on the CD track a few times. You may notice that the long notes are often held extra long (measure 4, 8, 11, 16, 20, 25 and 29). The longer notes exaggerate the tension of the song. Sing the tune with the CD. Play the tune without the printed music, as much of it as you can.

Remember to shift to second position before all of those "E"s on the A string. Use 2nd finger on the "D" immediately before the "E" in measure 3, 12, 15 and 24 of the printed music.

Down in the Willow Garden
Duet

Accompanying *Down in the Willow Garden*

The chords for this tune are the same as those for *Big Scioty*. Go ahead and review those scales and chords (♪♩ Example 17). The Cello 2 part for *Down in the Willow Garden* is an example of a more composed and varied style of accompaniment. Sometimes a tune is so beautiful or otherwise inspirational, you just have to work up a pretty accompaniment. This part was composed using the regular accompaniment style of combining roots, fifths and thirds (or tenths) and adding in complementary lines to the tune. Notice in measures 14 and 19 how the accompaniment follows the downward motion of the tune, harmonizing it a third below in pitch.

Try this part both bowed and plucked. You can also play an accompaniment using the roots of the chords or arpeggio style like that of the guitar on CD Track 30.

Improvising with *Down in the Willow Garden*

Ballads are great tunes for playing around with the melody. Because they are nice and slow, you can really experiment with varying the melody a bit. Keep the sound of the tune in your head while you play. I composed this example to maintain the original contour (with the melody going up and down in pitch) and effect of the piece.

 Track 29. *Down in the Willow Garden Variation*

Listen to the CD example a few times. Play it through and imagine that you have just composed this variation yourself. How can you change the notes? Would you like to hear something a bit different? Then play it!

♪♩ **Example 24**. *Down in the Willow Garden Variation*

Down in the Willow Garden
Variation

Make up your own variation of the melody for *Down in the Willow Garden* using the CD Track 30. Go back and use this same improvisational style on *Star of the County Down*.

Track 30. *Down in the Willow Garden* with guitar backup

Working with *Great Big Taters*

Great Big Taters is an old-time tune from the South and the Southwest. It's also known as *Great Big Taters in a Sandy Land*, or simply, *Sandy Land*. Whatever you call it, it's a fun piece to play and full of great syncopated rhythm.

 Track 31. *Great Big Taters*

Listen to the reference CD a few times and sing it through before you play this tune. A lot of notes are played a little sooner than you might expect! Notice that there is a *D.S. al Fine* printed at the end of this tune. This abbreviation for the Italian words *Dal Segno al Fine* means "go back to the sign (*segno*) and play until the end (*Fine*)". The sign is at the first measure and does not include the two pick-up notes – the end is at measure 16. Lots of music uses these Italian phrases, so you might as well learn what they look like and what they mean.

♫ **Example 25**. *Great Big Taters*

Great Big Taters

Accompanying *Great Big Taters*

There are only three chords in *Great Big Taters* – G, D and C. The tune itself is in G, so it uses the same scales as *Big Scioty*, just fewer of them! Now that you've played a variety of bass styles, you're on your own for this tune. Use whatever style you like. Feel free to change styles in the B and C sections of the tune (starting at measures 6 and 14 respectively).

Improvising with *Great Big Taters*

Because fiddles and cellos are tuned in fifths (chords also contain fifths) and many fiddlers play unaccompanied, lots of fiddle tunes can be harmonized by playing the tune with an open string. Just keep your bow over two strings at once and your left fingers curved so that you only finger one string. This example uses open strings the whole time. Listen to the accompanying CD and then try it out for yourself.

Track 32. *Great Big Taters with Open Strings*

Example 26. *Great Big Taters with Open Strings*

Great Big Taters
with Open Strings

What a great sound! Try this same technique on the second half of *Liberty*, playing on the D and A strings the whole time.

Play through the tune using one or more of the improvisational techniques that you have learned. Remember to use passages from the melody alternating with improvisational elements.

Track 33. *Great Big Taters* backup track

WORKING WITH *CRIPPLE CREEK*

Here's another old-time fiddle tune that I learned from my friend Jim Lewin. Jim is a great playing buddy; you should find one too. Most folks play this tune and there are many ways to play it. Here are three versions in a row.

 Track 34. *Cripple Creek*

The CD starts out with a very simple version (measures 1 through 8). Because *Cripple Creek*, like *Cherokee Shuffle*, is in A major (with F♯, C♯, and G♯), remember to keep your left hand in extended position (a whole step between your first and second finger – second and fourth finger play 1/2 step higher than usual) on the C, G and D strings.

♪♫ **Example 27**. *Cripple Creek Variations*

Cripple Creek
Variations

Variation 2

Improvising with *Cripple Creek*

If you haven't already, listen to, sing and play the first variation, starting at measure 10 (♩♩ Example 27) of *Cripple Creek*. It is more complex, with running eighth notes. Listen for the half step "slide" notes in the B section that we first used in the second *Rubber Dolly* variation. Also, the G♯ in measure 13 should be played in half position – nearer to the scroll.

The second variation starting at measure 20 is a bluegrass version of the tune. It is longer because the notes are varied on the repeats too. Notice the accented notes on the second and fourth beats in the second half of the tune. Bluegrass players often play more jazzy sounding versions of fiddle tunes.

 Track 35. *Cripple Creek* backup

Try an improvisation with CD Track 35 using the notes of the double stops in the Cello 2 part in the second version. Use the double shuffle technique (the third variation) from *Rubber Dolly* and see how that sounds. Do another improvisation using a combination of double shuffles and fragments from the tune.

Accompanying *Cripple Creek*

Since this tune is in A, the scales and chords are the same as those for *Cherokee Shuffle*. Go ahead and review those chords (♩♩ Example 7) if you need to. The bass accompaniment on the CD for the first eight bars of *Cripple Creek* (the tune) and from measure 20 on (variation 2) should be familiar to you by now. Listen closely to the second cello part starting at measure 9 (the first variation). It's played using an accompaniment style called *chopping*. This is a fun backup style but may be difficult to learn the first time you try. Just keep working at it and you'll get it.

The following written accompaniment for the second version of *Cripple Creek*, the tune in measure 10–19 (♩♩ Example 27) does not include the bass line (you can supply that on your own using any of the styles you have already learned) but does include the third and fifth of each chord played as double stops. This is the way that fiddle and mandolin players play backup.

You will also notice "X" notes on the third beat of each bar. These "Xs" stand for "chops", a percussive bow stroke on the string. Richard Greene, fiddler extraordinaire, invented the chop technique while playing in Bill Monroe's band. Chops imitate the rhythmic "chunks" of the mandolin.

Cripple Creek
Variation Two Accompaniment

INTERLUDE: CHOPPING

It is difficult to explain how to play chops without being able to demonstrate them to you, but here I go. Remember, chopping is a bow stroke. It uses a down-up, up-down-up pattern (*down bow* is when you pull the bow, *up bow* is when you push the bow). The third beat of the measure-long pattern is a down bow gone astray, just a little bit crunchy sounding. Try playing the pattern now. Try playing straight quarter notes, with the third quarter note crunching down for the chop effect. For some people, this will be enough to get you started and you can skip the next paragraph. Need more explanation? Then read on.

To play chops:
1. Straighten your bow-hand thumb. This is the only time it should ever be straight.
2. Keep your bow very close to the string.
3. Holding the bow, use a slight waving hand motion like you would if you were slapping a table top (but keeping your hand close to the table) or clapping your hands if your left hand was already resting (palm up) on your knee.
4. The chop should be placed very near the frog of the bow.
5. Once your chop makes contact with the string, the chop should also include a slight downward slide towards the bridge.
6. The down bow chop should "stick" to the string (because the weight of your hand is now digging into the string) and make an additional little sound when you let it up on the up bow. Try it out and see if you can imitate the sound on the CD. You can use chops with bass lines too.

WORKING WITH *THE ROAD TO LISDOONVARNA*

The Road to Lisdoonvarna is an Irish jig. I first learned it from Scott Walker, a fine Irish cellist from North Carolina. It's very well known and is a standard in Irish jam sessions. Listen to the CD track a few times to get used to the 6/8 rhythm. In 6/8 time there are three eighth notes per beat, so the dotted quarter note gets the emphasis. There are two dotted quarter notes per measure. Do the math and listen to the CD. Sing along with the CD until you can play most of the tune without the printed music.

The Road to Lisdoonvarna
Duet

Accompanying *The Road to Lisdoonvarna*

 Track 37. *The Road to Lisdoonvarna* chords, scales, and pentatonic scales.

Theory tip: this tune is in E minor. Notice that it has the same key signature (one sharp, F♯) as G major. Here are the chords, scales, and pentatonic scales that go with them. Remember, just as in *Big Scioty*, the pentatonic pattern is different for minor scales and major scales.

♪♪ **Example 30**. *The Road to Lisdoonvarna* scales

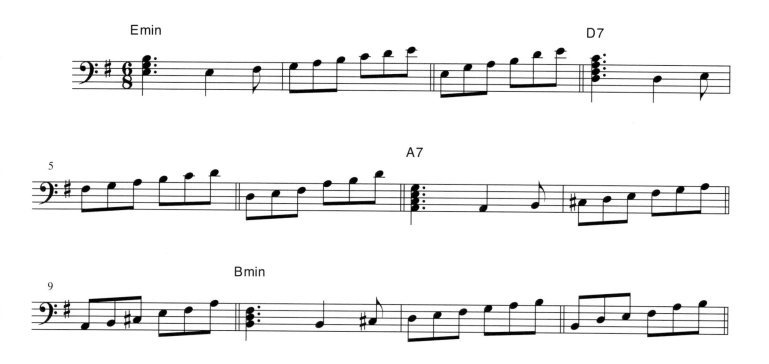

Most of the time, the tune of this jig has the rhythm of a quarter note followed by an eighth note for each beat – a long/short pattern. Since this is the main rhythm, it's best to accompany in the same style – and that's the way most Irish jigs are accompanied. I was fortunate enough to play with the great Irish guitarist John Doyle (we were accompanying Liz Carroll, the rhythm queen of Celtic fiddle music) and he also accompanies jigs this same way.

You can see and hear that the notes used are like the arpeggio accompaniment – the root on the first beat and the fifth and the third (played as a tenth) on the third eighth-note beat. The fifth and tenth can be played as *double stops* (two strings together). I usually move my left hand around in one unit: For major chords (like the D and A chords), first finger on the root and first and third finger on the fifth and tenth. For minor chords (like the E minor and B minor chords), first finger on the root and first and second finger on the fifth and tenth. But you can play around with the fingering to suit yourself.

Improvising with *The Road to Lisdoonvarna*

Irish music is not overly improvised – just a few notes are changed here and there after the third or fourth rendition of the tune. The following example is a harmony cello part, meant to complement the first part. Play all three parts together, or play the harmony part with the tune, or with the accompaniment. Try to compose your own harmony part, using the roots, thirds and fifths of the chords on the main notes and eighth-note connecting patterns when it seems appropriate.

Track 38. *The Road to Lisdoonvarna* with three parts

Example 31. *The Road to Lisdoonvarna Third Part*

You can also add grace notes to the tune, just as you did in *Star of the County Down*. Try adding grace notes before the longer notes – dotted quarter notes or quarter notes.

Interlude: Jams and Jam Etiquette

After learning the tunes and the accompaniments for at least five of these tunes, go out and find a bluegrass, Irish, or fiddle jam in your area. Ask around in the music stores that carry mandolins – almost every county has some sort of jam session going on. If it's out in a park under some trees, just be sure to bring your own chair!

The proper etiquette at a jam session is to play very quietly or over to the side if you don't know the tune. Listen for the roots of the chords so you can join in with the group playing backup (accompaniment) as soon as you have the chord progression down. Usually, beginners of all ages are welcome at these sessions. Fiddle jams are about the most inviting musical events you can imagine. Here in Santa Cruz, California, the weekly Sunday sessions attract folks of all ages – children just learning chords, young teenage go-getters, fine adult players, beginners in every age group, and a lot of frisbee-catching dogs.

Usually, people at a jam session will each suggest a tune as their turn comes in the circle. Be ready with your tune ideas in your head (make sure you can play the whole tune!) so that you can lead a tune when it's your turn. Never suggest a tune that you can't remember – it's much better to skip your turn.

If you can't find a jam session, throw your own party. Get together with some violinists and cellists (maybe you can find a guitarist and a mandolin player too!) and teach them the tunes you've learned. These tunes are meant to be played with other people and are the most fun when played that way.

Be aware that when you first go to a jam session you might get a few strange looks. After all, the cello is relatively new to this style. Be prepared for a couple of teasing remarks: "Is that a little bass?" or, "That's a really big fiddle!" They'll be delighted once you start to play because the cello sounds GREAT in all fiddle ensembles.

Working with *Elzic's Farewell*

Elzic's Farewell is a traditional tune that Darol Anger taught me when I told him I was working on this book. It's in three parts, and the third part is the pay-off – a real rocking number. After listening to the track a few times and singing it as well, try to play through the tune without the printed music. Try learning it in chunks – first the A section, then the B section, and finally the C section. If you use the printed music, in measures 10, 11, 14, and 15 be sure to shift to second position with an extension between your first and second fingers (the C and D).

Elzic's Farewell
Duet

56

Accompanying *Elzic's Farewell*

Elzic's Farewell is in A minor, the same key as *Star of the County Down*. Review the chords and scales in *Star of the County Down* if you need to – A minor, C, G, and E minor (♪♩ Example 12). *Elzic's Farewell* also uses the chord and scale of D, which should be as comfortable as an old shoe for you by now.

In Cello 2 I have used a different type of accompaniment for each section of *Elzic's Farewell* – first just the chord roots, then the bass line double shuffle, and finally the bluegrass bass with fifth and tenth double stops.

 Track 40. *Elzic's Farewell*, guitar backup

Using CD Track 40 to practice with, feel free to change the order of accompanimental styles, to replace them with other styles or to use the same style throughout the tune. Listen carefully to decide which accompaniment style allows each section of the tune to shine. Which accompaniment styles seem to add tension to the performance? Which ones relax? Which ones best complement the tune? There is no right answer, just your own opinion.

Improvising with *Elzic's Farewell*

Play the C section starting at measure 18 up an octave using CD Track 40 (the backup track). Does playing in the higher octave help this section stand out better? Try replacing some of the measures in that section with pentatonic scales, chordal arpeggios or with rhythmically different ideas. See how you like each variation. Try recording yourself and listen for what works and what doesn't.

WORKING WITH *THE EIGHTH OF JANUARY*

This is an old-time fiddle tune that has been recorded by lots of great players. I heard old-time fiddler Bruce Molsky (he's not old though!) play this tune and was just blown away. Bruce plays it with a real Appalachian flair, but the version here is a little tamer in style. The name of the tune refers to the date of the 1815 Battle of New Orleans, when Major General Andrew Jackson led a small army to victory against the British. This tune was set to lyrics in 1936 by a history teacher/musician and topped the pop charts in 1959 as *The Battle of New Orleans*.

Get the sound of the tune in your head by listening to CD Track 41 as many times as you need to until you can sing along with the melody. It's nice and short, so give it a try.

Track 41. *The Eighth of January*
♪♩ **Example 33**. *The Eighth of January*

The Eighth of January

Accompanying The Eighth of January

The Eighth of January is in the key of D major, the same as that of *Liberty* and *Fisher's Hornpipe*. It uses the same chords and scales. For this tune, I like to use chops or bluegrass bass accompaniment. Experiment with a few different accompaniments and see which one you like the best. The recorded example uses a bluegrass bass.

Improvising with *The Eighth of January*

This variation is in bluegrass style. The A section uses more eighth notes and the contour of the tune is just a little different. Darol Anger taught me this variation.

Track 42. *The Eighth of January* bluegrass variation

Example 34. *The Eighth of January "A" Section Variation*

The Eighth of January
"A" Section Variation

Track 43. *The Eighth of January* backup

Try improvising in a similar fashion to the bluegrass version (A section variation) using eighth notes instead of quarter notes in the second section. Just play the melody notes plus notes one step above or below the quarter notes you are replacing. Try using pentatonic scales in alternation with phrases from the original tune. Remember, there are only three different key areas in this tune.

Working with *Shebeg, Shemor*

This is a famous old Irish tune composed in the seventeenth century by the great Irish harper Turlough O'Carolan. It is also known as *Sidh Beag Aus Sidh Mohr or Sheebag and Sheemore* as well as various other spellings of the tune name. My long-time friend, multi-style fiddler Chris Vitas, taught me this one in San Diego. Listen to the tune a few times before you sing or play it. Always try to play through the tune without using the printed music. You will develop your listening skills and your ear-to-hand coordination.

Track 44. *Shebeg, Shemor Duet*

♪♩ **Example 35**. *Shebeg, Shemor Duet*
(You will find this example on the next page.)

Shebeg, Shemor
Duet

Accompanying *Shebeg, Shemor*

Shebeg, Shemor is in the key of D. It uses the same chords and scales as *Fisher's Hornpipe*, with the addition of B minor, a chord and scale found in *The Road to Lisdoonvarna* (♪♩ Example 30). Review these chords and scales. Use the bass accompaniment methods you have already learned for slow waltzes. Try out the waltz accompanimental styles that you learned with *Star of the County Down*. Long bass notes or bass notes with double-stop fifths and tenths work very nicely, as does the arpeggio accompaniment.

 Track 45. *Shebeg, Shemor for 3 cellos*

After an extended period of listening to her CDs in the car, I fell in love with the gorgeous Irish fiddle sound of Liz Carroll's compositions and realized how beautiful three-part arrangements of Irish tunes could be. As in the parts for *The Road to Lisdoonvarna*, I wrote Cello 2 and Cello 3 parts to complement and support the tune. Here is a middle cello accompaniment part

♪♩ **Example 36**. *Shebeg, Shemor – Cello Two*

Shebeg, Shemor
Cello Two

Improvising with *Shebeg, Shemor*

Improvise a melody for *Shebeg, Shemor* that changes the contour or melody of the tune just a bit. As with *Down in the Willow Garden*, keep the sound of the original tune in your head while you play. Try another improvisation that uses the Irish ornaments that you learned for *Star of the County Down*. Now use both improvisational ideas; add Irish ornaments to your own tune idea. Play sections of *Shebeg Shemor* an octave below. Record your ideas and listen to them. Do you like what you hear? Would you like to change something? These are your own ideas and it's all up to you.

 Track 46. *Shebeg, Shemor* backup

WORKING WITH *SAINT ANNE'S REEL*

This is a tune that is frequently called at jam sessions. It's a good one to have under your fingers. In preparation for learning the tune, listen to CD Track 45 many times. Make sure you can hum along, and then see how much of it you can play without using the printed music. Since it is in the key of D major (two sharps, F♯ and C♯), make sure that you use extended position on the G and C string (a whole step between your first and second finger so that your second and fourth finger play 1/2 step higher than usual). This rule applies whenever you play on those lower two strings.

 Track 47. *Saint Anne's Reel*
♫ **Example 37**. *Saint Anne's Reel*

Saint Anne's Reel

Accompanying *Saint Anne's Reel*

This rollicking tune will sound good with just about any type of accompaniment that you've learned. Try out a variety of styles using the same style throughout the tune, or changing styles for the B section, or even changing at the repeat. What sounds best to you? You don't need to have just one answer; you can change styles as often as you like.

If you need to, review the D major scales and chords in *Liberty* (♩♩ Example 2) as well as E minor and B minor in *The Road to Lisdoonvarna* (♩♩ Example 30)

Improvising with *Saint Anne's Reel*

I first learned the A section of this tune an octave higher, and I suggest that you try it that way too. Try out a version using pentatonic scales. Review the D major pentatonic scale in *Fisher's Hornpipe*, find the E minor scale and chord in *Big Scioty* and the B minor scale and chord in *The Road to Lisdoonvarna*. Try a version alternating pentatonic scales with the double shuffle rhythm. The tune is bowed using the shuffle style. Try rebowing *Saint Anne's Reel* so that your bow strokes sometimes change on the off-beats. Try playing fewer or more eighth notes per bow. See what kind of rhythmic accents you can generate with your changing bow strokes.

 Track 48. *Saint Anne's Reel* backup

Here is my "twin fiddle" part for *Saint Anne's Reel*. The twin fiddle style is a thought-out accompaniment to the tune that usually harmonizes a third or a sixth above the original tune, and exactly matches its pitch contour. I have heard fiddlers Buddy Spicher, Billy Contreras and Randy Elmore spend hours figuring out twin fiddle parts to tunes. What an inspiration! You'll need to shift in the "B" section. Add fingerings if you need them.

Track 49. *Saint Anne's Reel* with twin cello part
♩♩ **Example 38**. *Saint Anne's Reel – Twin Cello*

Saint Anne's Reel

Twin Cello

WORKING WITH *THE GIRL THAT BROKE MY HEART*

My friend Ben Blechman insisted that I learn this Irish reel and I finally did after hearing Darol Anger play this killer rendition of it at a concert in the redwoods up in Ben Lomond, California. Thanks Ben!

Listen carefully to the CD Track 50. Notice that the second full statement of the tune uses a variation in the "B" section. Sing along with the track, then play it. Don't forget to play without the printed music if you can.

Track 50. *The Girl That Broke My Heart*

Shift to third position in measures 3 and 7 and play the D, E and F with your first, third and fourth fingers. In the "B" section variation (♫ Example 40), shift to 2nd position at measure 4, using extended position 1st and 4th fingers for the C and E.

♫ **Example 39**. *The Girl That Broke My Heart*

The Girl That Broke My Heart

Accompanying *The Girl That Broke My Heart*

The Girl That Broke My Heart is in the key of G and uses only the chords of G, C and F. Review the G and C chords and scales in *Big Scioty*, and find the F chord and scale in *Star of the Country Down*. This tune sounds great with a rock-and-roll type bass. Using CD Track 51, try the *Big Scioty* accompaniment style, Cello 2 (♪♩ Example 15). Try playing just the eighth-note roots with Charleston and double shuffle accents. Don't forget to change chords on the half measure when needed. Try out other accompaniment patterns as well. It's always more satisfying to have a variety of options available to you.

 Track 51. *The Girl That Broke My Heart* guitar backup

Improvising with *The Girl That Broke My Heart*

When thinking about different ways to improvise over a tune, it's always a good idea to use characteristics of the tune itself. The B section, starting at measure 10 (♪♩ Example 39), of *The Girl That Broke My Heart* uses arpeggiated patterns. The B section variation in (♪♩ Example 40) uses a different arpeggio pattern, but still has that broken chord feel. I learned this variation from Darol Anger.

♪♩ **Example 40.** *The Girl That Broke My Heart "B" Section Variation*

The Girl That Broke My Heart
"B" Section Variation

Try out your own ideas using phrases from the tune or variations on the tune that interest you. Try adding grace notes to some notes as you did in *Star of the County Down* (♪♩ Example 14).

WORKING WITH *BILL CHEATHAM*

Bill Cheatham is a fiddle and bluegrass tune that has been played a lot of different ways. This version is a little more modern than most, making ample use of arpeggios. Darol Anger played this version for my friend Ben Blechman who taught it to me. Listen to and sing with the tune before you play it.

 Track 52. *Bill Cheatham*

Because it is in the key of A major, make sure to use your extended hand position for the D, G, and C strings. Otherwise those fourth finger F♯s, C♯s and G♯s might sound strange and out of tune. In the second half of measure 3, shift to 3rd position. Use extended position between your first and second fingers so that you can play the whole step between D and E. Shift back to 1st position on the B in measure 4.

♩♪ **Example 41**. *Bill Cheatham*

Bill Cheatham

Accompanying *Bill Cheatham*

This A major tune uses the same scales and chords as *Cherokee Shuffle*, without the F♯ minor (Example 7). I like to use the arpeggio accompaniment pattern illustrated in *Liberty* (cello 2, Example 1), but try out a lot of different styles as well. Watch out for the B section with its many chord changes. You may like to use the bluegrass bass style there (playing just the roots since the chords change so frequently).

Improvising with *Bill Cheatham*

 Track 53. *Bill Cheatham* backup

Because this tune also uses arpeggiated chords in the melody, try using some of the same strategies that you learned with *The Girl That Broke My Heart*. Use arpeggios starting with different notes or in a different order. Try using the first three notes of each scale in the B section; make up a little pattern that you can use, starting on the root or third. Play through these ideas slowly at first, until you can work them up to tempo.

WORKING WITH *FIRE ON THE MOUNTAIN*

Track 54. *Fire on the Mountain*

Fire on the Mountain has been played by lots of musicians for a really long time – Morris dancers in Britain, fiddlers in the Appalachians, and rock and rollers in various bands. Listen closely to this version on the CD, as it uses a really nice syncopated slur technique, the *Georgia Shuffle*. This bowing consists of a very short and fast down bow on beats 2 and 4 in order to accent the offbeats.

Keep your left hand in extended position on the G and D strings for the A section, and in extended position for the G string for the B section. Watch out for the G♯'s in measures 4, 8, 9, and 19. Make sure you play them in half position (closer to the scroll).

Example 42. *Fire on the Mountain*

Fire on the Mountain

75

Accompanying *Fire on the Mountain*

This tune can be accompanied any way that you like. It's in two different keys, the A section is in A major (three sharps, F♯, C♯ and G♯) and the B section is in D (two sharps, F♯ and C♯). There is very little chord change activity, so a more syncopated style might be better to use. On the other hand, the tune itself is quite syncopated so you might prefer a simpler style. Listen to the bass part on CD Track 52. Notice that the cello is playing a kind of bagpipe drone with long notes. Start this drone-style bass with a grace note a half step below the root. Try out all of the methods you have learned and see how you would like to accompany this tune.

Improvising with *Fire on the Mountain*

Since there are really only two key areas in *Fire on the Mountain*, A in the first section and D in the second section (making sure to change back to A major at measure 17 in the B section), the sky is the limit for improvisation. That is why this tune has been very popular with jam bands. On CD Track 53, we play through the entire tune twice to give you more room to jam. Try out arpeggio patterns, pentatonic patterns, and scale patterns. Try keeping the same general contour of the tune – starting with similar pitches and going up and down where the tune does. Try putting in syncopated rhythmic accents and using different bowings. Try improvising for a while and then playing the tune for a while. Record your ideas.

 Track 55. *Fire on the Mountain* backup

WORKING WITH *TAM LIN*

I learned the very old Irish tune, *Tam Lin*, from some of my cello students here in Santa Cruz. They learned it at Celtic camp from Celtic fiddler Deby Benton-Grosjean. Listen to the CD a few times to get a feel for this Irish reel. Sing with the track and then play it through without looking at the printed music.

Track 56. *Tam Lin* duo with guitar
♪♩ **Example 43**. *Tam Lin* Duet
(Please see this example on the next page.)

Tam Lin
Duet

Accompanying *Tam Lin*

Tam Lin is in the Key of D minor. As with all minor tunes, there are a variety of minor scales that can go with the tune. Here are the chords and scales for *Tam Lin*. Notice the four different minor scales for D minor, as well as the two different scales for the C chord. What are the differences between the minor scales? The two C scales? Check out the tune. Do you see the different scales here? Look at measures 10, 11, and 13. Notice the C sharp and B natural. You can use whichever scale you wish to accompany and improvise on *Tam Lin*.

Track 57. *Tam Lin* chords and scales

Example 44. *Tam Lin* chords and scales

The second cello part in (Example 43) uses more of a rock-and-roll type bass rhythm. You can also use any other accompaniment style that you wish. If you get together with other cellists, try using a variety of styles at once. That sounds great!

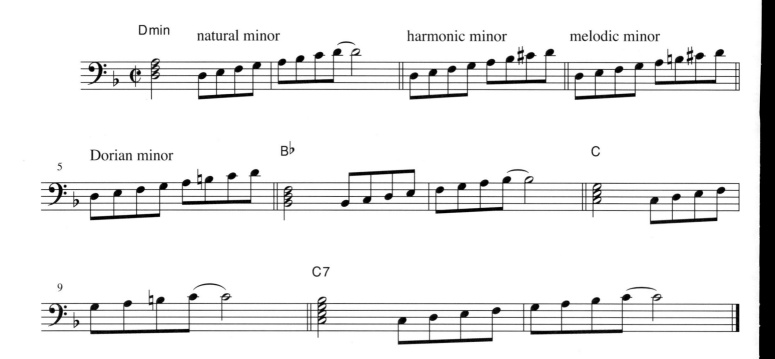

Improvising with *Tam Lin*

 Track 58. *Tam Lin* backup

This tune is often performed first at a moderate pace, then a faster one, a faster tempo still, and then as fast as everyone can possibly play it. As with all Irish tunes, the melody itself is not changed too much in performance. Just a note here or there may be substituted. Try an improvised chorus changing as few notes as possible, but still using some of your own ideas. Try another improvisation using your own melodic ideas. You can just stay in the key of D minor if you wish.

CLOSING THOUGHTS

Fiddle tunes are an important part of American musical history. They were, and continue to be, a huge influence on jazz and all popular music. Because the cello is new to fiddle tunes – at least in this century – it's helpful to remember that our role is not standardized. We can play the tunes AND the bass lines AND the accompaniment part. We can lend support to a fiddle player and share an equal role with a guitarist.

By learning the tunes and the different types of accompaniment that go with them in this book, you have developed many of the skills that you need to learn and accompany new fiddle tunes. By listening to the various CD tracks and learning to play without the music, you have begun the process of learning to play tunes that you hear by ear – no printed music needed.

Don't forget that most fiddle tunes have only a few different chords in them – and there are only a few keys that fiddle players use. So learning a good foundation of scales and chords in a handful of keys will really pay off.

All of you are forging new paths – get out there and form a band!

RENATA BRATT

Cellist and clinician Renata Bratt is president of the International Association for Jazz Education String Caucus where, together with Darol Anger and Martin Norgaard, she has served as a Resource Team Leader. She is also a member of the American String Teachers Association/National School Orchestra Association Alternative Style Festival and Awards Committee. She writes articles on improvisation for *ASTA* and the *American Suzuki Journal* and is a former president of the Suzuki Music Association of California. She arranged and recorded Dix Bruce's *BackUp Trax: Old Time & Fiddle Tunes for Cello* (MB20100BCD) for Mel Bay Publications. In addition to concertizing with various classical, jazz, and fiddle groups, Ms. Bratt has performed as a backup musician for such luminaries as Jimmy Page and Robert Plant, David Sanborn, Lyle Lovett, and Dionne Warwick. *Rolling Stone* magazine dubbed her an "ace performer" for her recording and touring work with alternative rocker Cindy Lee Berryhill's Garage Orchestra. Ms. Bratt received her Ph.D. in Music from the University of California at San Diego.